Cougars,

Panthers, & Mountain Lions

Nature's Perfect Hunter

Dr. Richard A. NeSmith

Love of Nature Series

ISSUE 30

Applied **P**rinciples of **E**ducation & Learning

APE-Learning *Publications*

dr.nesmith@gmail.com

http://richardnesmith.obior.cc

MAY 2025

DEDICATED to my son, Ricky, whom I just learned, loves cougars!

ISBN: 9798594276444

FLESCH-KINCAID GRADE LEVEL: 8.8

Cougars, Panthers, & Mountain Lions
(family Felidae)

Cougars, panthers, and mountain lions are all common cats named for the same species, Puma *concolor*. They are *non-roaring*, wild, elusive, and highly adaptive **mammals**. This also includes those wildcats referred to as pumas, painters, red tigers, and catamounts. Cougars belong to the family **Felidae**. As far back as 1851 A.D., naturalist **John Audubon** concluded that cougars in both North and South America were indistinguishable.

This North American cat has more *names* than any other animal. The *Guinness Book of World Records* recorded 64 different **common names**. Common names are generally local in nature and often create such confusion. However, some of the blame can be explained by there being, at one time, thought to be dozens of species.

Carl Linnaeus[1] formalized the taxonomic identification of plants and animals into the accepted modern scientific system of naming organisms.[2] He proposed the genus-species "felis *concolor*" to describe a big cat with a long tail

---

[1] (1707- 1778) was a Swedish botanist, zoologist, taxonomist, and physician.

[2] This is now sometimes known as **binomial nomenclature**, because all organisms are named down to a *genus* and a *species* based on Linnaeus' rules. Note: the species' name is always italicized. Following species is subspecies, which is also italicized. Subspecies are, generally, able to interbreed though often do not.

for cougars. The cougar is known technically by the scientific name "Puma *concolor*" or "felis *concolor*." *Concolor* refers to the cat being *of one color*.[3]

Following Linnaeus' scientific description of cougars,

researchers once listed **32** zoological subspecies. By the late 1980s, with the assistance of genetic and DNA comparison, this was reduced to just seven.[4] Most of the subspecies'

---

[3] *Concolor* means: of the same color or faction; of uniform color throughout; of similar color.
[4] As a result of a genetic study conducted in 2000, most biologists now believe there is *no real difference* between the cougar family's Western and Eastern branches.

genes were too close to be considered separate. By default, these became divided into sub-species, which can interbreed but typically do not generally due to geographic separation.

These subspecies[5] include:

> Puma *concolor coryi*: Florida, United States
>
> Puma *concolor cougar*: North America
>
> Puma *concolor costaricensis*: Central America
>
> Puma *concolor capricornensis*: eastern South America
>
> Puma *concolor*: northern South America
>
> Puma *concolor cabrerae*: central South America
>
> Puma *concolor puma*: southern South America

When writing about these cats, scientists now generally refer to them all as ***pumas***. This study will focus on North America's two subspecies, the Puma *concolor coryi*, and the

Note the historic range in light green and the current range in dark green.

Puma *concolor cougar*. We will refer to them both as cougars, recognizing that those living in Florida have been given the

---

[5] phylogeographic groups (phylo - form meaning "race," "tribe," "kind"), used in phylogeny (the branch of biology that deals with phylogenesis, or how an animal is related to other animals).

local name, Florida Panther.

These cats once roamed the Americas freely. Native Americans called the puma *nosh doytsa,* the spirit of the mountains. Early North and South American explorers referred to them in their Spanish language as **León** or lion. Or *gato monte,* meaning cat of the mountain, thus our common *mountain lion.* On the other hand, **cougar** appears to be from an old South American word *cuguacuarana,* shortened to the word "cuguar" and later the modern "cougar" spelling.

We will see that these animals are some of the most beautiful and attractive animals, yet can also take down an animal seven times its size. Cougars, being smart, elusive, strong, and swift, may well be **Nature's Perfect Hunter**.

Range

At one time, the North American cougar (Puma *concolor*

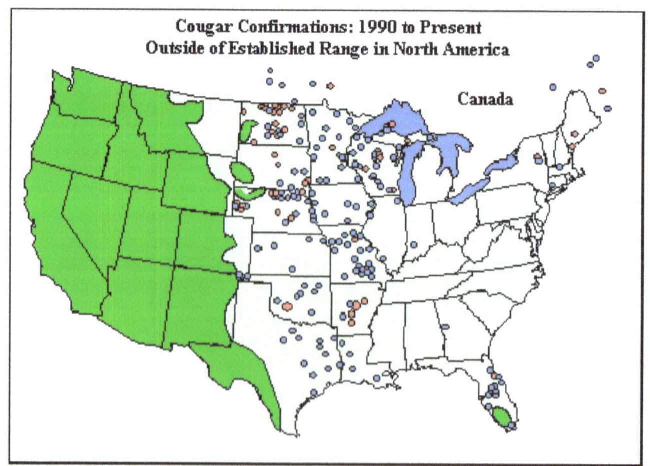

Cougar Known Range and Confirmations
Green = established populations
Blue = Class I Confirmation
Red = Class II Confirmation

cougar) was one of the most widely dispersed land mammals in the Western Hemisphere (see map on page 7). They existed from the Atlantic to the Pacific Ocean.[6] From the Canadian Yukon down to the southern tip of Chile. Its historical range extended from Maine south to Georgia,

west into eastern Missouri and eastern Illinois, and north to Michigan and Ontario, Quebec, and New

Brunswick, Canada. However, the last official record of a **breeding population** of cougars in the upper northeastern United States and Canada was in 1932 (New Brunswick) and 1938 (Maine).[7] Vermont reported its last cougar sighting as early as 1881, while Tennessee as late as 1930. (See map on page 8).

Cougars virtually have no natural enemies, sit at the top of the food chain, and are considered **apex predators**, ruling their domain. But with modern civilization, that would all begin to change. Cougars quickly dwindled in numbers due

---

[6] Alaska is considered outside the range of cougars, and no cougars have ever been observed in Hawaii.

[7] Occasional sightings of cougars have occurred outside their noted ranges, however, those are often individual cats and not breeding populations. Isolated individual cougars found outside their range may present some evidence of expansion, however, generally this is not the case as to really expand requires propagation and the establishment of a breeding population.

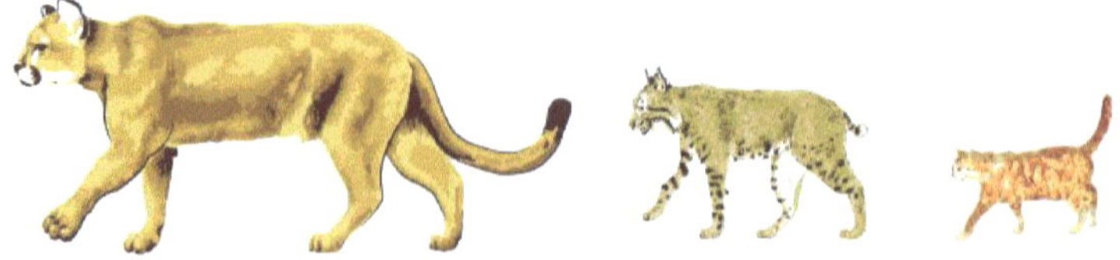

to sports hunting and extermination during the early founding colonies on the American East Coast. Cougars were continually forced to retreat.

Being a rather sizeable opportunistic hunter who stalks its prey, one can only imagine encountering this cat as frightening and intimidating to the early settlers. As seems to be a common practice, people tend to kill off anything we, as humans, feel threatens our existence.

As westward expansion continued, they would find their populations dwindling and their range shrinking. It was definitely the case in the 1700s, 1800s, and even 1900s

when many cougars were **extirpated**[8] from most of the eastern range.

Between 1910 and 1978, cougars were considered **vermin** and often blamed for some deaths and threats to people and livestock they had not committed. And, for some, they had. Bounties were placed on their heads to eradicate them from the environment. During that era, more than 50,000

cougars were killed for bounty or sport.[9]

It is now believed that cougars have been eliminated from about two-thirds to three-fourths of their original range. In all likelihood, the eastern cougar was extinct by the 1930s. It was genuinely a **mass extinction**! However, the eastern cougar was announced as extinct in 2011, but a new

---

[8] Rooted out and destroyed completely in their habitat. The eastern cougars were probably extirpated in the southeast from Alabama in the mid-1800s.

[9] Some historical documents indicate that as early as 1764 AD Jesuit priests in California offered a live bull in return for a dead cougar.

breeding population has been re-established in Florida.[10] Some people are already stating what an ecological success this intervention has been.

However, the Florida venture is still too small of a population and territory. It is too soon to know the outcome to begin celebrating. Besides, the current space of 3500 square miles (9,064 sq. km) may not be large enough to make a significant difference. The Florida population is small and unable to expand further north at this time, much less refilling their historical southeastern range.[11]

Today, cougars continue to populate most of the west, including the long corridor from the west coast down to

---

[10] The U.S. Fish and Wildlife Service formally removed the eastern cougar from the endangered species list and declared it to be extinct in 2018. Note: The Endangered Species Act (ESA) authorizes only two federal agencies to identify species as either threatened or endangered. For most marine species, that agency is the National Marine Fisheries Service of NOAA or the National Oceanic and Atmospheric Administration in the U.S. Department of Commerce.

[11] Seldom mentioned is the fact that the Florida Panther's range is *dynamic* and literally fluctuates with the season and tides and rising sea levels. In addition, possible plans to establish cougar colonies in Arkansas, Georgia, and northern Florida have not come to fruition.

southern South America. However, some have fittingly named them *phantoms of the prairie.* More recently, they are being noted as the *ghosts of the Rockies.*

Today, viable **breeding** cougar **populations** are found in just sixteen states: Washington, Oregon, California, Nevada, Arizona, Utah, Idaho, Montana, Wyoming, Colorado, Nebraska, New Mexico, South Dakota, North Dakota, Texas, and Florida. The current number of cougars in North America, however, has been nearly impossible to know.[12] However, it is estimated to be around 30,000 animals throughout the American West.[13]

Researchers have been unable to provide an exact estimate regarding how many cougars are in the wild. Generally, the

---

[12] There appears to be no extensive data on cougar populations in respective states, however, this may be in the making. See: https://www.cougarfund.org/state/arizona/

[13] Cougarfund.org noted that "All western states with surviving cougar populations (except Texas) established limited protections for the cats by the early 1970s. Today cougars are classified as a game species and hunted for sport in the thirteen states of: Washington, Oregon, Nevada, Arizona, Utah, Idaho, Montana, Wyoming, Colorado, New Mexico, South Dakota, Texas, and North Dakota. In these states, authority for setting and carrying out hunting programs is held by each state's wildlife management agency." Available at: http://bit.ly/2XuSb9C

density of cougars ranges from one to seven cats for every 62 miles (100 km) of territory, with males permitting

several females to be present in their ranges. Oregon
estimates that its cougar population is around 6,600, while

California believes it has between 4,000 and 6,000

animals.[14]

In Florida, the number of eastern cougars/panthers is estimated to be from 120 to 250 adults. Ontario, Canada, reported an estimated 550 pumas in their province.[15] Canadians are hopeful that their numbers are increasing steadily to a sustainable population.

Characteristics

A cougar's body is similar to a house cat but on a larger scale. Cougars have relatively small heads but can average five to nine feet (1.5-2.7 m) in length from head to tail. They weigh from 100 to 225 pounds (45.3-102.5 kg), with males weighing as much as 50 pounds (22.7 kg) more than

---

[14] California, which also provides the cougar the most protection, claims to have the highest western population. However, that number is not verified by the current data. California appears to be the only state that prohibits hunting them.

[15] See: https://www.researchgate.net/publication/229473609_Doubting_Thomases_and_the_Cougar_The_Perceptions_of_Puma_Management_in_Northern_Ontario_Canada

females.

The cat's rear limbs are slightly longer than the heavily muscular forelimbs, enabling cougars to leap tremendous distances vertically and horizontally. They can jump forward 40 feet (12.2 m).[16] Such lunges quickly surprise unexpected prey. This large cat can jump 18 to 20 feet (5.5-6.1 m) straight up in the air from a standing position. That's more than three times the height of an average person! They can reach speeds of up to 50 miles per hour (80.5 kph) for short distances.

Cougars vary in color from reddish-brown to yellowish-brown (deerlike) to gray, with a lighter coat underneath and a black tip on their long tail. Most have black markings on the ears and face, which provides a personalized means of identification. Though the coloring and markers vary to some degree, they blend in with their particular surroundings. Cougar newborns, called **cubs** or **kittens**,

---

[16] one of the highest-jumping animals in the world

are spotted until they are 4-5 months old. These patterns may remain up to 14 months of age.

Like house cats, cougars do **purr** but cannot roar like lions or tigers. Unlike house cats, cougars not only like water but are excellent swimmers and climbers. During hot days cougars will spend a significant part of their day cooling off in and around water, swimming, playing, or just relaxing. Crossing a river is seldom a deterrent. Especially for the

Florida panther, commonly swims between islands and bay heads, searching for prey.

Grooming is essential and natural for cougars, just as it is for all cats. Grooming helps keep their coats clean. The bumps on a cat's tongue are tiny **spines** called **papillae**. They use their rough tongues, much like we would use a hairbrush, remove any loose hair, and untangle any matted fur. Female cougars groom their babies frequently, and

young siblings have been seen grooming one another.

Sight

Of the cougars' senses, **vision** is the strongest, which helps them hunt. A cougar can see color, enabling them to see prey from far away. Their **eyesight** is so sharp that it can detect the slight movement of a mouse in the grass. Their pupils allow them to see at night almost as well as in the daytime. Their ears can move around, so they **hear** sounds on all sides. These senses aid the cougar in avoiding danger and finding prey, thus helping them to survive.

Large eyes close together at the front of the head provides a superior sense of depth perception. Cougars have a wider range of **vision** than humans, seeing 285 degrees compared to our 210. This difference is due to having more **rods** (for night vision) than **cones** (for color vision). On the backside of their eyes, the **retina**s are highly sensitive to low light levels. Behind the rods is an additional cell layer called the

The Flehmen response is the cougar's ability to curl the upper lip to activate the vomeronasal organ (VNO), an olfactory-chemosensory organ located between the roof of the mouth and organ, to help him smell the pheromones and other scents in the air.

tapetum lucidum, reflecting light entering the eyes back to the eye for an enhanced night vision effect.

This reflection membrane can be demonstrated by shining a bright light into a cougar's (or a house cat's) eyes and seeing the glow (**eyeshine**) in the dark. In the daytime, cougars typically have dark brown eyes. When the light reflects at night, the eyeshine will glow a bright yellowish.

Smell

They also have a strong sense of **smell**. A cougar's sense of smell is better than a human's but not as good as a dog's. After sniffing a spot where another cougar has urinated, a mountain lion will display a *lip-curling grimace* known as a **Flehmen response** (see photo above). This behavior allows them to use a sensory organ in the roof of their mouth to better "read" the scent (**olfactory**). Male cougars may use the Flehmen response when smelling a female lion's urine to determine whether she is ready for mating. A female hormone scent will stimulate his urge to mate.

Hearing

We know very little about a cougar's ability to hear. The ears are rounded, and the back of the ears are solid black to dark gray. The outer ear includes the pinna (the part visibly made of cartilage and covered by skin, fur, or hair) and the ear canal. The pinna (which do not have ear tufts as do bobcats) is shaped to capture sound waves and funnel them through the ear canal to the eardrum. In cats, the pinnae are mobile and can move independently of each other.

The cougar depends more on vision and hearing when hunting but can track deer and other prey's scent trail. Smell probably plays a more significant role in finding a mate. Cougars, it seems, also seem to share the domestic

cat's attraction to catnip.[17]

Touch

Also, like house cats, cougars have a face full of whiskers (**vibrissae**). These extra hairs typically grow along with the cat's nose, cheeks, chin, brow, and wrists. Cat whiskers provide a sense of touch. They are full of *sensory nerve endings* called **Merkel cells**.[18] These cells serve an essential purpose for nocturnal hunters. Cougars have some of the most sensitive facial hairs of all animals.

Nerve-ending clusters at the base of each whisker in the **epidermis** detect changes in airflow and currents. The sensory receptors provide awareness of nearby objects,

---

[17] This was first noticed as an attractant when big cats swarmed around withered or bruised plants growing in the wild. A full response to catnip involves four actions, usually in this order: Sniffing, licking, and chewing with head shaking.

[18] All vertebrates, including humans, have Merkel cells in their skin with the highest concentration can be found in mammalian whiskers.

whether prey or potential predator. These whiskers (**vibrissae**) are also located on the cat's wrists, sensing movement close to the ground, increasing paw movement and accuracy. The importance of this may be that these facial vibrissae sensors help cougars orient their *fatal bite* as it captures and kills the prey.

Habitat

Cougars are highly adaptive mammals and live on plains, desert regions, mountain ranges, forests, and swamp areas. They develop or learn behaviors that help them survive in their specific habitat. However, due to habitat loss and fragmentation, the Puma *concolor coryi* stayed east of the Mississippi River, becoming more isolated from the western species.[19] Finally, they began to disappear

---

[19] Housing projects, parking lots, golf course, and expansion malls do not make very good additions to a cougar's home range, but they do remove habitats where aniamals and potential prey would live. With human commodities come traffic and super highways, air pollution, noise pollution, water pollution, and toxins, all of which reduce or kill wildlife.

altogether. They make their home anywhere there is shelter and prey, but some ecosystems have more significant challenges than others.

There are likely many places in eastern North America with adequate habitat to support populations of cougars.[20] Though the western cougar population may now be expanding, it is unknown whether cougars will continue to expand their range eastward. With human densities in eastern North America continually increasing, the return of a top-level predator such as the cougar will depend on public awareness and acceptance. Should the general public continue to view them as *vermin,*[21] then the likelihood of returning to their historical range is slim to none.

These wildcats require large adjoining areas with adequate

---

[20] It has been estimated that theoretically 10,300 cougars could easily populate their historic eastern region.
[21] This was the word that early settlers used to describe cougars, degrading them as lowly rats and mice.

large prey to meet their social, reproductive, and energy needs. They require a great deal larger ranges than any other wild species in North America. Cougars seem to do very well living in parts of the country that feature steep canyons, rim rocks, and dense brush for protection.

Diet

As a top-tier predator, cougars are obligate[22] **carnivores** and need ten pounds (4.5 kg) of meat per day. Though they are restricted to meat, they are not picky eaters. However, they prefer fresh kills rather than scavenging dead carcasses. They are generally not **scavengers**, but should the opportunity come along they might do so.

As a ***generalist*** hunter, it will make a meal of any animal it can catch. The key to the hunt, however, is ***stealth***. This works well because most cougars prefer night hunting (**nocturnal**). Cougars rarely chase their prey. They are

---

[22] True carnivores, meaning they do not consume any other type of food except meat.

masters of camouflage and will slowly and silently creep forward and then pounce. In contrast, others appear to be more active at dusk and dawn (**crepuscular**), and some will hunt during daylight. A cougar's preferred food includes deer, mountain goats, elk, wild sheep, moose, and other hoofed animals.

To state that cougars are one of the best hunters is supported by the fact that though not selective about what they catch, they are highly selective about how and where they hunt. Being stalkers, they hunt in heavier cover and have a flexible selection. This means they often select prime-condition prey. One researcher reported an **82 percent success rate** while hunting elk and deer. In comparison, cheetahs have a 58 percent success rate, while leopards have a 38 percent rate. Even wolves who frequently work in packs only have a successful kill rate of 14 percent.

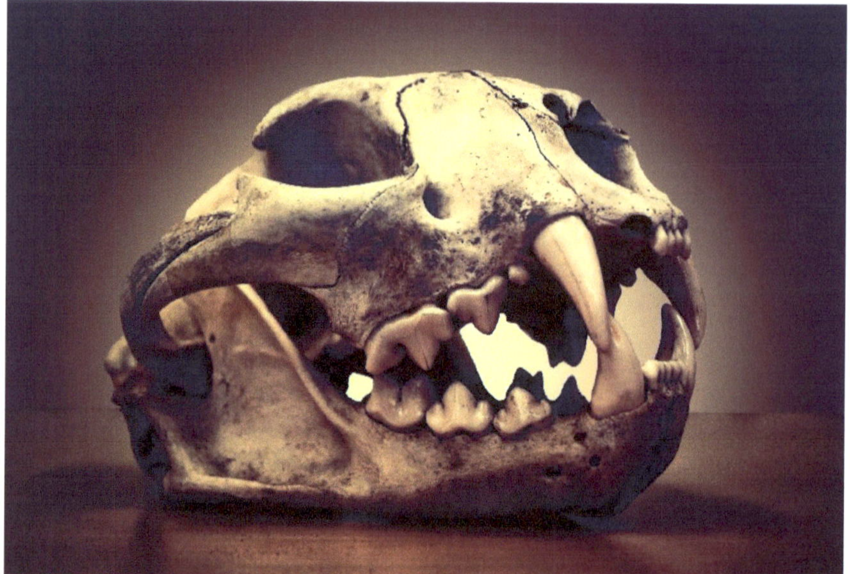

Deer seems to be their favorite food,[23] and this fact troubles some humans who enjoy hunting. However, it will also eat wild hogs, coyotes, and badgers, along with raccoons, armadillos, rabbits, hares, beavers, wild turkeys, other birds, and small rodents. Florida panthers sometimes will catch alligators. As opportunists, they will also prey upon domestic pets and livestock, including chickens, goats, sheep, and cattle. Under stressful seasons, cougars have been known to eat the smaller prey, including insects.

With the ability to take down prey far beyond their size, they can feed for days on a single catch. A very large deer can end up being a meal for one or two weeks. They will hide or bury the carcass, called **caching**, so other predators cannot steal their meal. Though at the top of the food chain, they occasionally compete with other predators,

---

[23] Some estimate that a single cougar could kill 259 deer over an average 6-year lifespan, which is about 43 deer per year.

including bears and wolves, for food.[24] Sometimes wolf packs will also attack and kill cougars.[25]

Skilled and crafty hunters, hiding in the bush, behind rocks, and ambushing their prey with powerful hind legs, they deliver a deadly neck bite using the **carnassial teeth** located on the sides of the jaw[26] They can break their prey's neck with one strong bite, severing the spinal cord and causing almost immediate death, driving prey to the ground, with teeth and retractable claws extended.[27] (See illustrations below and on page 30). The cougar's ability to leap, run, and jump makes escape nearly impossible.

Behaviors

Solitary, mysterious, and magnificent are perfect descriptions for these cats. They prefer to be alone and do not even tolerate their own, except during mating season. Cougars can be fierce and very aggressive with their

Mountain Lion

Dog

Front Paw

Hind Paw

---

[24] These two groups are more scavenger-minded, thus more interested in taking over a kill since it is easier than hunting their own.

[25] In a one-on-one battle, a cougar will usually survive the fight. Wolves, however, as packs, are more likely to affect cougars by dominating the same territory and taking advantage of prey opportunities. Wolves can also disrupt the cougar's ability to reproduce.

[26] There are large upper premolar and lower molar teeth of a carnivore, adapted for shearing flesh. They are used to inflict the killing blow to the prey by severing the spinal cord, crushing the windpipe or severing a major artery.

[27] Claws are retractable, so there are no *claw marks* in a cougar's footprint.

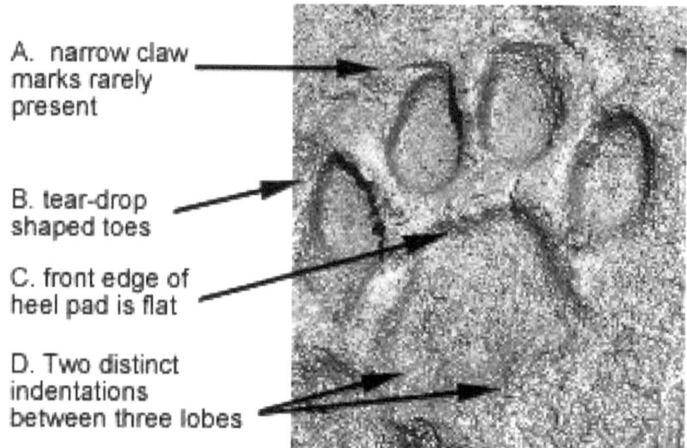

territory, marking boundaries and strategic ranges with scent glands, urine, and feces. Territories can shift, such as in regions where deer and elk migrate.

They will protect their territories and will fight other cougars, even to death.[28] They hiss, growl, and scream, and can easily rip their prey to shreds. The number of fatal human attacks in the last 100 years in North America number 125, of which 27 have been fatal. However, deadly cougar attacks are very rare. Such cougar attacks occur less frequently than fatal snake bites, lightning strikes, or even fatal bee stings.[29] Children and pets are the most vulnerable and easily targeted when unaccompanied.

Cougars **prefer to avoid humans** and stick to their own patches, as long as they are not unduly disturbed.[30] However, this isolation is becoming increasingly grim as human populations move further and further into the wild. Cougar populations do, however, seem to be in decline due

---

[28] Intraspecific – fight between species.
[29] A person is 700 times more likely to be killed by lightning than to be attacked by a cougar.
[30] Some have suggested of other animals that they fear humans more than humans fear them. For the cougars there is some evidence that suggest that a cougar fears human voices more than any other natural thing.

to **habitat fragmentation**.

Though most animals communicate with sounds, cougars do very little, except for mating and interacting with offspring. Nursing cubs emit high-pitched, birdlike chirps and cries. Some communication that occurs between the mother and her cubs also includes chirping sounds to call wandering offspring. Whistles, growls, purrs, and squeaks are some of the few sounds cougars can make. Still, older cougars rarely do, relying mostly on body language, scent-

marking, and avoidance.

Living alone and keeping to themselves is the rule rather than the exception. Cougars are secretive and hunt, often under cover of darkness, but can be quite active between dusk and dawn. Encountering a cougar in broad daylight is unlikely, but not impossible. Most will spend daylight hours sleeping and resting in small, hidden places.

Compared to the females, male cougars are a bit on the

wild and untamed side. Males can be ferocious, vicious, and very territorial. They are solitary most of their lives except for breeding periods, which can last a couple of weeks per year. Though their territory may overlap with females, there is occasional contact, but not in an amicable manner. She may even fight him if she is raising cubs. And, she may even fight to the death over dead prey.

It is a rare occasion if a male and female share a kill. The female will establish herself around the territories of strong male cougars. Those within this "circle" do some socializing but very little with those outside it. These cats usually avoid inhabited areas. Those raised in captivity and released tend to be ill-equipped to survive genuinely. These cougars, being accustomed to people, create problems for themselves and the public.

Reproduction

Males cougars are ready to breed at about 36 months of age

and the females at 24 months. Some studies have indicated that females have mated as young as 20 months. The actual age at which a cougar first breeds often depends upon her establishing a home range. A significant breeding challenge that cougars face is finding a mate due to their solitary lifestyle. These cats are usually scattered across hundreds of miles of rough terrain.

Another complication cougars must overcome in reproduction is that a female may only be receptive to mating several days out of a month. Mating is quick, repeated, and often fierce. During the estrous cycle,[31] females vocalize when seeking a mate, and scent markers make a hormonal announcement in their urine. With their keen sense of smell and communication, they indeed find a mate (**monogamous**), and some find several mates

---

[31] Estrus a recurring period of sexual receptivity and fertility in many female mammals; heat.

(**polygamous**).[32]

When a mate is located, cougars breed vigorously for seven to eight days by *copulating* 50 to 70 times within 24 hours. What might be *courtship* to them often looks like a catfight to us. Mating can be quite loud (**caterwaul**[33]) but lasts less than a minute. All of this is necessary to cause the female ovaries to release an egg (*induced* **ovulation**) for fertilization.[34]

These cats interact only to **mate**, which can happen at *any time of year* (called **polyestrous**). However, there appears in some regions to be a preferred season of delivery (*birth pulses*).[35] Females give birth from one to six young. However, two or three kittens is the average. Once pregnant, she will run the male off and retreat to a secluded den. She will then raise the young while the males return to their solitary lifestyles.

Female **gestation** lasts 88-96 days before the young are

---

[32] Cougars do not mate for life with a single male, but whether a season involves a one male or several may be a result of the availability of males in a given range.

[33] a shrill howling or wailing noise like that of a cat

[34] No ovulation occurs unless the vagina and cervix of the female are stimulated repeatedly during mating. Induced ovulation is when a female animal ovulates due to an externally-derived stimulus during, or just prior to, mating, rather than ovulating cyclically or spontaneously. Stimuli causing induced ovulation include the physical act of coitus or mechanical stimulation simulating this, sperm and pheromones.

[35] Though polyestrous, it appears that in many parts of their enormous range they may favor certain times of year for raising litters. Female pumas (Puma *concolor*) give birth in all months of the year with a possible birth pulse in July– September. This pulse is proposed to be timed to provide increased survival probabilities to young born during these months. Such "birth pulses" are more common and closer linked to higher-latitudes, which have more severe and rapid seasonal changes. Young born in July–September the subsequent year.

born. By that time, they will have located a safe but simple place to den. When cougar kittens are born, they do not open their blue eyes for two weeks. Newborn cougar cubs usually weigh just over a pound at birth. Within 10 to 20 days, they grow to double their weight, and by the time they reach two months of age weigh as much as nine pounds.

Time in the den alone is a vulnerable and dangerous period  for cubs who can fall prey to wolves, coyotes, or even other male cougars.[36] The kittens must be quiet and still when the mother goes out hunting when they stop nursing and are ready to eat food. Should a female lose her kittens to predators or other circumstances, she may begin her estrous cycle and breed again soon after the loss.

When cougar babies are born, their coats typically have black and brown spots, which camouflage them from predators. The spots generally last for about six months.

---

[36] It has been documented that males do indeed kill and even eat kittens on occasion.

Baby cubs are born helpless, deaf, blind, and almost immobile, making them vulnerable to predators. Within minutes of being born, kittens will begin nursing. To gain strength and learn how to take down their prey, cougar cubs play and pounce on one another.

The mother cougar keeps the kittens safe by grooming them to keep their newborn smell from attracting predators

and moving them from den to den. The risk of becoming prey for the young cubs is great, with a **survival rate** between 50 to 66 percent. Approximately one kitten survives per litter (**mortality rates**). And nearly one-third of juvenile cougars are killed by other cougars. After all, risks are factored in only 8 out of 100 juvenile cougars live to establish their own home ranges.

After three months, the cubs are sufficiently weaned and

begin to accompany their mother to visit kill sites. The female often takes meat to her cubs until she weans them two to three months old. Eventually, the female will leave them at a kill site for several days at a time while she hunts for their next meal. Mother cougars will travel further in search of food as their cubs become older and stronger.

Though kittens can live independently after six months, such as when the mother dies or is killed, this appears rare. Soon they will be hunting alongside her. They will track and hunt with their mother for two years, allowing them to hone their hunting and survival skills and giving them time to develop their *killing bite*. These lessons determine life or

death. Approaching the second year, they will be run off by their mother. Some travel far distances to establish their own territory, as cougars need a lot of room to roam.

Because cougars generally bear young every other year, a female cougar who lives for 8 to 10 years may produce five litters. According to reports, one mother cougar in captivity could have seven litters in 16 years. Female cougars are highly aggressive with raising young and are more likely to attack to protect their little ones.

Miscellaneous

Nature exists in a delicate **equilibrium**. Each species participates in the local *circle of life*. As an apex predator, cougars play a massive role in helping the ecosystem at large and the habitat in which they live to remain balanced. Even the left-over carcasses from their kills feed over 200 different species of birds and mammals, not including the insects that follow. Removing one species of animal or plant from a habitat can have a tremendous effect on that system's health.

Four significant threats to cougars: ❶ natural events, ❷ automobiles, ❸ genetic isolation, ❹ depredation, and ❺ poisons.

Natural Events

Like any animal in the wild, the cougar faces many natural

events, including
starvation,
wildfire, freezing
cold, snow, and
daily dangers,
including
predation to
fungal, bacterial,
or viral diseases.
Most animals are

equipped to survive for many years but eventually, die from the toll. Nature has a way of *policing* itself. These, however, are natural. It is the unnatural causes that we have to seek to moderate.

Automobiles

Automobiles are highly dangerous for cougars, which become more so when housing and new roads are built. Crossing roads takes the life of wildlife at an unacceptably high number. Highways also isolate and separate some cougars. In many locations where there are a larger number of cougars, engineers have successfully provided underpass corridors. Some of these engineered **corridors** have shown a 98 percent decrease in animal fatalities. These passageways ensure safety crossing roadways. But it also permits a variety and a variation of the **gene pool** from other species populations.

Genetic Isolation

Animals that become cut off from other like species, whether naturally or geographically, create issues involving the genetic pool. Most **genetic diseases** and deformities are **recessive** traits. When a gene pool is limited, then inbreeding occurs.[37] This causes those recessive genes to produce traits that show up physically, physiologically or both.

When one species becomes isolated, the number of **genetic variances** is reduced. This situation creates health and survival issues, not to mention reduces the ability to adapt or overcome any new bacterial or viral encounter. New genetic lines are needed for a population to remain healthy.

Depredation

Suppose a cougar becomes a severe threat, and there is evidence of livestock predation. In that case, ranchers and farmers often can

obtain a *legal permit* to remove or euthanize wildlife, including cougars. A depredation permit will allow one to capture and kill that particular cougar that killed their livestock.[38] Identifying which cougar is guilty is often impossible to do. Cougars do not see humans as **prey** but as something *different*.

---

[37] Called *inbreeding depression* and leads to a high risk of extinction.
[38] In California, an average of 98 mountain lions have been killed each year with depredation permits.

Poisons

Some animals often cause farmers issues such as taking livestock, which causes some to put out poisons. Rats and mice are often the target of many poisons that aim to cause death by internal bleeding (*anticoagulant rodenticide*). The problem with these is that other carnivores consume these dead rodents. If it doesn't kill the consumer, it accumulates in the blood system, slowly poisoning the animal and eventually the ecosystem.

Cougars tend to have a high-risk lifestyle, frequently exposed to stress, injury, or death, but not an uncommon consequence for one that often hunts animals much physically larger than themselves. Attacking elk, deer, or moose is a dangerous feat. Being kicked, trampled, or head-butted causes injuries, not to mention being gored by horns or antlers. If you have not viewed the snow leopard falling off a cliff while holding onto a ram (on YouTube), you need to see this.[39] Then, there are other natural dangers, including lightning strikes, poisonous snake bites, and rock slides.

A healthy cougar in the wild can live to around ten years of

---

age. In captivity, cougars can live as long as 20 years.[40] Females seem to have a shorter lifespan, possibly due to the stress of reproduction and raising cubs.

Cougars are protected and legally classified as "specially protected species." Also, 47 states have laws preventing one from owning a cougar or other wild exotic animal, as well as protecting and hunting wildcats. It is currently estimated that more than 1,000 cougars are held in private captivity in the eastern United States. However, additional cougars are likely kept as pets without authorization.

Some confusion and inaccuracies still prevail today due to

---

[40] There is a report of one captive cougar that lived to be 29.

fairy tales and various media cartoon creations that black panthers exist. North American ***panthers are never black.***[41] What is often mistaken for a black panther is a

---

[41] African leopards, also referred to as panthers can rarely have black offspring, but only about 11 percent of leopards globally are black.

melanistic **leopard** or **jaguar**.[42] **Melanistic**[43] refers to an increased amount of dark pigmentation in the skin or fur. Cougars (of the puma genus) are all of the tan, yellow/reddish color, not black.

What to do if you encounter a cougar

Statistically speaking, you are far more likely to be attacked by your neighbor's dog than a big cat. Cougars do not hunt humans, nor are they "man-eaters." In nature, they are shy and usually avoid humans at all costs. Though they do not see people as food, they do see us as trespassing in their territory. Keep in mind that cougars are stealth hunters, so if one is going to attack you, you probably *will not see them coming*. In reality, if you see one, they are probably NOT stalking you.

Cougars do, by instinct, recognize small stature, irregular or rapid movement,[44] or defend a domestic animal (that looks like prey) to be indicators to attack or kill. The issue often becomes the question of perception for *what humans view as pets* that *cougars view as prey*. Whether a cat, dog, or goat, these become unnatural targets for cougars. Cougars will *help themselves* to dinner, not realizing that is unacceptable behavior. Here are ***seven precautions*** and suggestions.

1. Know in advance whether you are in cougar country, and be prepared and alert during your visit. This would mean avoiding hiking ***alone*** in these areas.[45] Groups are far safer and seldom endangered.

---

[42] The jaguar is the largest cat found in the Americas, and the third largest in the world (only the tiger and lion are larger). There are currently estimated to be 64,000 jaguars in North America. Most are found from the southwestern United States to Central America. This population has continued to decline over decades.
[43] Melanism is a mutation that results in completely dark skin. It is the opposite of albinism. The word "melanism" is deduced from a Greek word that means black pigment.
[44] Also referred to as animated behavior, as in lively and is showing feelings.
[45] It is ill-advised to bring a house pet to an areas of known cougar traffic.

❷ Stay calm, remain standing. Avoid *direct* eye contact (look at the cougar's feet, instead). Make yourself appear larger, holding up and flaying your arms in the air, then back away slowly.

❸ If the cougar does not leave immediately, then make motions and loud noises. Some have indicated that cougars are quite frightened of human voices.

❹ If the cougar is still watching (stalking), make loud noises such as yelling, hollering, blowing a whistle or an air horn.[46] Throw objects at it.

❺ Give the cougar a way to escape. Do not ever stalk, antagonize, or corner any wild animal, and certainly not a cougar.

❻ Running is ill-advised, and not only can you *not* outrun a cougar, it is also a natural sign triggering a cougar to chase down its prey.[47]

❼ If you must defend yourself, use your hiking sticks, trekking poles, or solid clublike branch to keep the cougar at bay, poking as needed.

Cougar attacks are rare, and fatal attacks are even more so. Realizing that you may be viewed as a *trespasser* and not a cougar's lunch can help you understand that what you are witnessing is defensive rather than offensive. If you have a child present, keep the child next to you as a wildcat will focus on the smallest member.[48]

---

[46] Some recommend carrying bear spray, but carrying a small portable air horn is also an excellent tool to scare off any wild animal and come in various sizes for under $20. See:
https://www.amazon.com/gp/product/B00450FLAU/

[47] Running and rapid movements can trigger the animal's instinctual prey response and it will easily chase you down.

[48] Sixty-four percent (64%) of the few human attacks are children.

Some cougar biologists in the United States are encouraged, believing that the nation's cougar population may be rebounding. Whether we can live and co-exist peacefully together in harmony will probably decide the fate of the cougar. Helping to protect their habitat and range is vital to whether these animals survive or become extinct. They are beautiful and serve an essential role in the ecosystem, yet they are **Nature's Perfect Hunter**.

Special thanks to wildlife and nature photographer Randy Johnson for this beautiful illustration.
http://johnsonartworks.com

REVIEW

1. What are the common names for the cats discussed in this book?

2. Why do common names often creating confusion?

3. What is a *subspecies,* and how does it apply to cougars?

4. What kinds of noises do cougars make to communicate?

5. How far and how high can these large cats jump?

6. How much territory do a male and a female cougar need to survive?

7. How social and close are cougars with other cougars?

8. How do cougars get food, and why is it fair to say *they do not chase their prey*?

9. What do you think makes the cougar such an effective hunter?

10. What is the Florida Panthers' population, and what needs to be done to *enable* them to expand their home range?

COUGAR

COLORING PAGE

http://www.supercoloring.com/coloring-pages/cougar-head

Name:_______________________

Cougars, Panthers, & Mountain Lions: Nature's Perfect Hunter

Read the clues or statements then carefully record your answers in the spaces provided. Use the Word Bank if needed.

retractable   polyestrous   solitary   deer   vision   eyeshine   papillae   cashing

fragmentation   pumas   nocturnal   kill   gestation   survival   estrus

Across

2. If you can't eat it all after a kill then you simply bury it, called ______

3. Cougar's greatest sensory is?

4. Cougars, are also panthers, mountain lions and ______

7. Period of time a female cougar is pregnant.

8. Habitat _________ seems to be the reason most cougars and Florida panthers are dying off?

10. Since cougars are not very social animals, they are said to be ______

12. With a ________ rate between 50 to 66 percent, cougar cubs often never reach adulthood.

13. Cougars are great hunters and have an 82 percent success or _____ rate.

14. Animal which cougars seem to be very fond of hunting?

Down

1. Proper term for the whiskers on a cat's face, legs, or feet.

4. What is the word used that indicates a female can be ready to breed at any time?

5. Cougar footprints do not reveal claws because they are ?

6. The time when most cougars are active about or hunting?

9. Shine a light in a cat's face at night and you see a reflection.

11. Time in which a female cougar is ready to mate?

INTERESTING SOURCES TO CONSIDER

Black Bears & Florida Panthers 09-22-19. Available at: https://youtu.be/SGY19po-idQ

By the Numbers: Saving the Florida Panther. Available at: https://youtu.be/t-TiDWndD-4

California Mountain Lions: The Legends of California. Available at: https://youtu.be/GLvRuSjSYgo

Co-existing with the Florida Panther. Available at: https://youtu.be/rIqWFw6OvXg

Coyote vs. Cougar. Available at: https://youtu.be/iN2rVI-VvbM

Dual Cougar Attack in Northern Alberta. Available at: https://youtu.be/YvzOBrzGpYw

Endangered Species: The Florida Panther. Available at: https://youtu.be/Jz2GkxAnRDM

Florida Panther Encounter in the Big Cypress area of the Everglades. Available at: https://youtu.be/U7AQKGSJWKw

Florida Panther Encounter. Available at: https://youtu.be/tlbhWparKJg

Florida Panther Surprises Woman On a Nature Walk On a Boardwalk. Available at: https://youtu.be/bQiqxSc0lIU

Florida Panther: All You Need To Know About This Cougar. Available at: https://youtu.be/JE4PjH1OZoM

Florida Panthers Duel in The Devil's Garden. Available at: https://youtu.be/yjyMv3B3j9Q

Information about Cougars. Available at: https://youtu.be/1eJto7VlNOc

Mountain Lion Stand Off With Hiker. Available at: https://youtu.be/rNO2CUGPSl8

Mountain Lion Track Identification Available at: https://youtu.be/0YGUoQ4LVTc

Puma Lion. New Full National Geographic. Available at: https://youtu.be/9Xbzm0KnYp8

The Rocky Mountain Lions. (Wildlife Documentary).Real Wild. Available at: https://youtu.be/5EAQxnIHUCU

ABOUT THE AUTHOR

Richard NeSmith is a native of Florida, USA. He grew up wading through the swamps of central Florida with his two younger brothers  during the pre-Disney era, and unknowingly, falling in love with biology, wildlife, and nature. He has lived in seven American states, twice in Australia, and once in Mexico City. He holds eight university degrees and has taught for 14 years in secondary schools, here and abroad, and another 13 years as a professor in several American universities. His service includes professor of science education, Dean of Education, Campus Dean, as well as an online instructor. His passion for learning (and *how we learn*) did not develop until *after* graduating from high school. His only explanation for this is that *having a goal made all the difference in the world.* He enjoys reading, hiking, nature photography, golf, tennis, and R.V. camping.

http://richardnesmith.obior.cc

Applied **P**rinciples of **E**ducation & Learning *presents*

APE-Learning

AMAZON AUTHOR's PAGE:

https://www.amazon.com/author/richardnesmith

Educational, wildlife, and naturalist books
Dr. Richard NeSmith.

Issue 1
Raccoons:
Friendly Bandits
Dr. Richard NeSmith

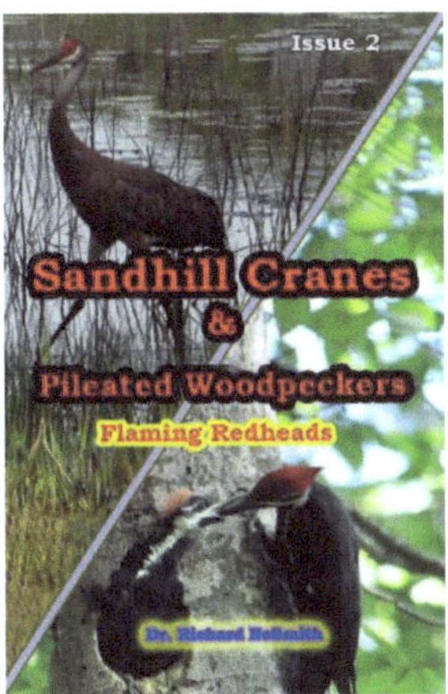

Issue 2
Sandhill Cranes
&
Pileated Woodpeckers
Flaming Redheads
Dr. Richard NeSmith

Issue 3
American
Alligators
&
Crocodiles
Dr. Richard NeSmith

Issue 4
Bobcats:
Ghostly Elusive
Dr. Richard NeSmith

Issue 5
Foxes:
Sneaky Rascals
Dr. Richard NeSmith

Issue 6
Armadillo:
Little Armored One
Dr. Richard NeSmith

Issue 7
Squirrels:
Bushy Tail Scampers
Dr. Richard NeSmith

Issue 8
River Otters:
Aquatic Clowns!
Dr. Richard NeSmith

Issue 9
Beavers:
Nature's Engineers!
Dr. Richard NeSmith

Issue 10
Black Bears
Titans of the Forest
Dr. Richard NeSmith

Issue 11
Freshwater
Turtles
Dr. Richard NeSmith

Issue 12
FUNGI, LICHENS
& MUSHROOMS
Dr. Richard NeSmith

Paperbacks: http://amazon.com/author/richardnesmith

e-books: https://bit.ly/3iuCgB3

---

[i] **Special thanks to the following who kindly provided permission to use their photographs.**

From Unsplash: Andy Holmes, Allan Bueno, Thomas S., John Borrelli, Wilson Chen, and Bruce Jastrow.

From Pixabay: Wayne Linton, Ian Lindsay, Icewall42, Mike Goad, Mike Hansen, M. Maggs, Rudeboy5, Al Seeger, and Justie K.

Finally, *special thanks* to likeminded friends who love wildlife and who willingly shared their wonderful photos, and many of whom have become my friends: **Stacey Diamond**, **Cindy Frasier**, **Gail Halm**, **Randy Johnson** *and* **Greg Jowers**.

JOHNSON ARTWORKS (http://johnsonartworks.com/)

If you enjoyed this book, please go to amazon.com and share a nice review. 😊

Thank you everyone.

Love Learning – Love Nature – Love Life